EXPLORING SPACE

Jupiter

by Derek Zobel

Consultant:
Duane Quam, M.S. Physics
Chair, Minnesota State
Academic Science Standards
Writing Committee

BLASTOFF! READERS
3

BELLWETHER MEDIA · MINNEAPOLIS, MN

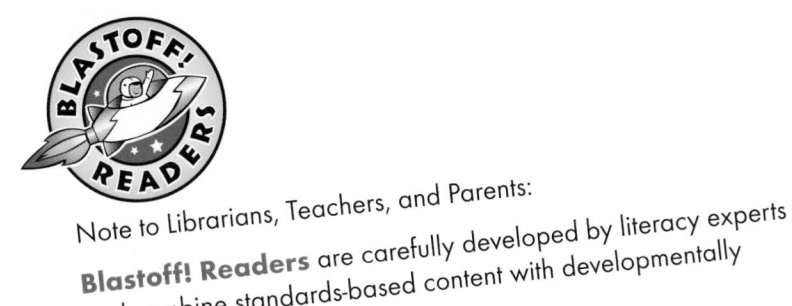

Note to Librarians, Teachers, and Parents:

Blastoff! Readers are carefully developed by literacy experts and combine standards-based content with developmentally appropriate text.

Level 1 provides the most support through repetition of high-frequency words, light text, predictable sentence patterns, and strong visual support.

Level 2 offers early readers a bit more challenge through varied simple sentences, increased text load, and less repetition of high-frequency words.

Level 3 advances early-fluent readers toward fluency through increased text and concept load, less reliance on visuals, longer sentences, and more literary language.

Level 4 builds reading stamina by providing more text per page, increased use of punctuation, greater variation in sentence patterns, and increasingly challenging vocabulary.

Level 5 encourages children to move from "learning to read" to "reading to learn" by providing even more text, varied writing styles, and less familiar topics.

Whichever book is right for your reader, Blastoff! Readers are the perfect books to build confidence and encourage a love of reading that will last a lifetime!

This edition first published in 2010 by Bellwether Media, Inc.

No part of this publication may be reproduced in whole or in part without written permission of the publisher. For information regarding permission, write to Bellwether Media, Inc., Attention: Permissions Department, 5357 Penn Avenue South, Minneapolis, MN 55419.

Library of Congress Cataloging-in-Publication Data

Zobel, Derek, 1983-
Jupiter / by Derek Zobel.
  p. cm. – (Blastoff! readers. Exploring space)
Includes bibliographical references and index.
Summary: "Introductory text and full-color images explore the physical characteristics and discovery of Jupiter. Intended for students in kindergarten through third grade"–Provided by publisher.
ISBN 978-1-60014-406-6 (hardcover : alk. paper)
1. Jupiter (Planet)–Juvenile literature. I. Title.
QB661.Z63 2010
523.45–dc22   2009037990

Text copyright © 2010 by Bellwether Media, Inc.
Printed in the United States of America, North Mankato, MN.

010110   1149

Contents

Jupiter is a **planet**.
It is a **gas giant**.
It is named after
the **Roman god**
of thunder.

Jupiter is the largest planet in the **solar system**. It is 88,846 miles (142,984 kilometers) across.

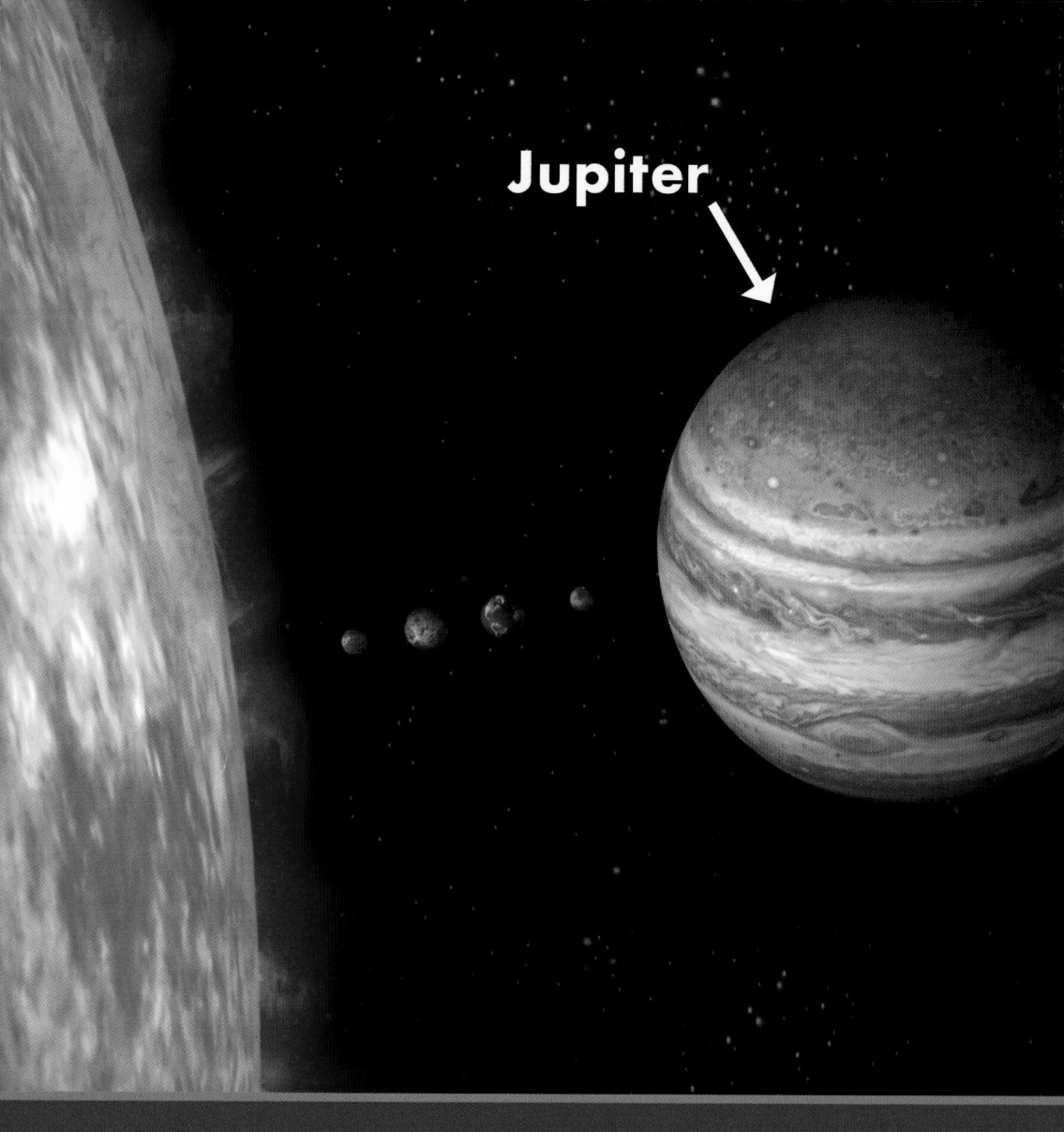

Jupiter

Jupiter is more than double the size of all the other planets combined!

Jupiter is the fifth planet from the sun. The sun is about 484 million miles (779 million kilometers) from Jupiter.

All of the planets in the
solar system **orbit** the sun.
The amount of time it takes
a planet to orbit the sun
is one year.

Jupiter

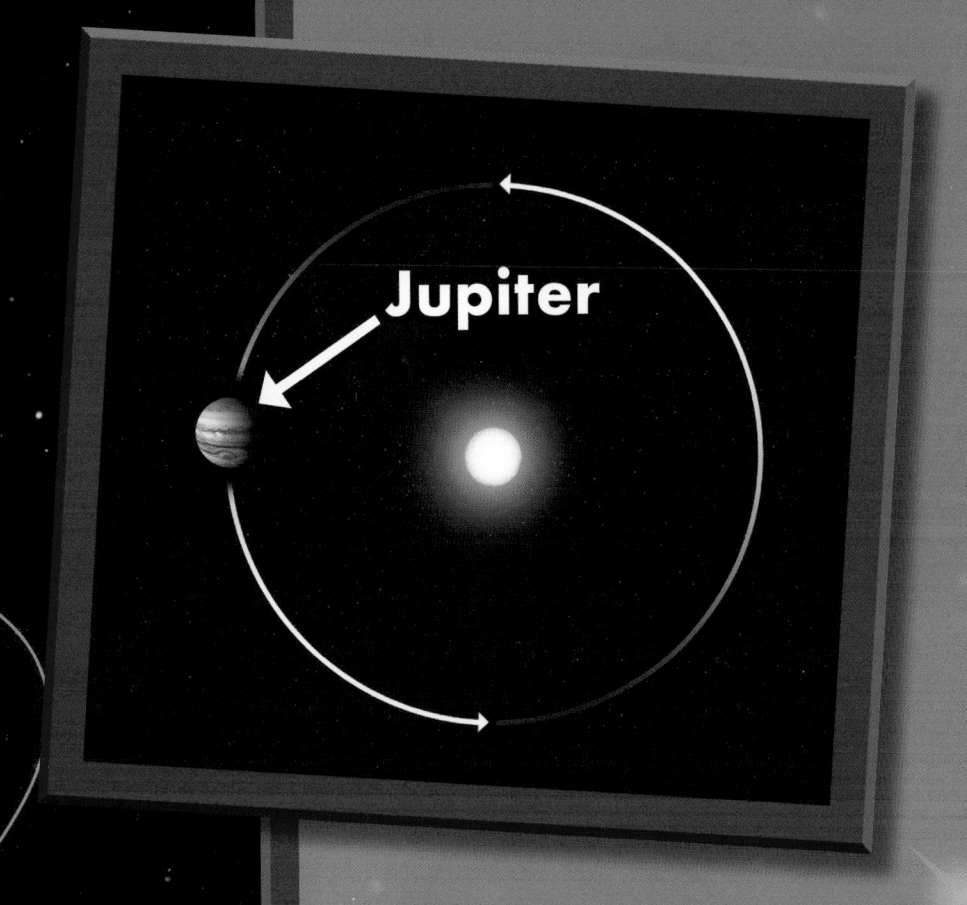

Jupiter

Jupiter has a long year. It takes almost 12 Earth years for Jupiter to orbit the sun one time.

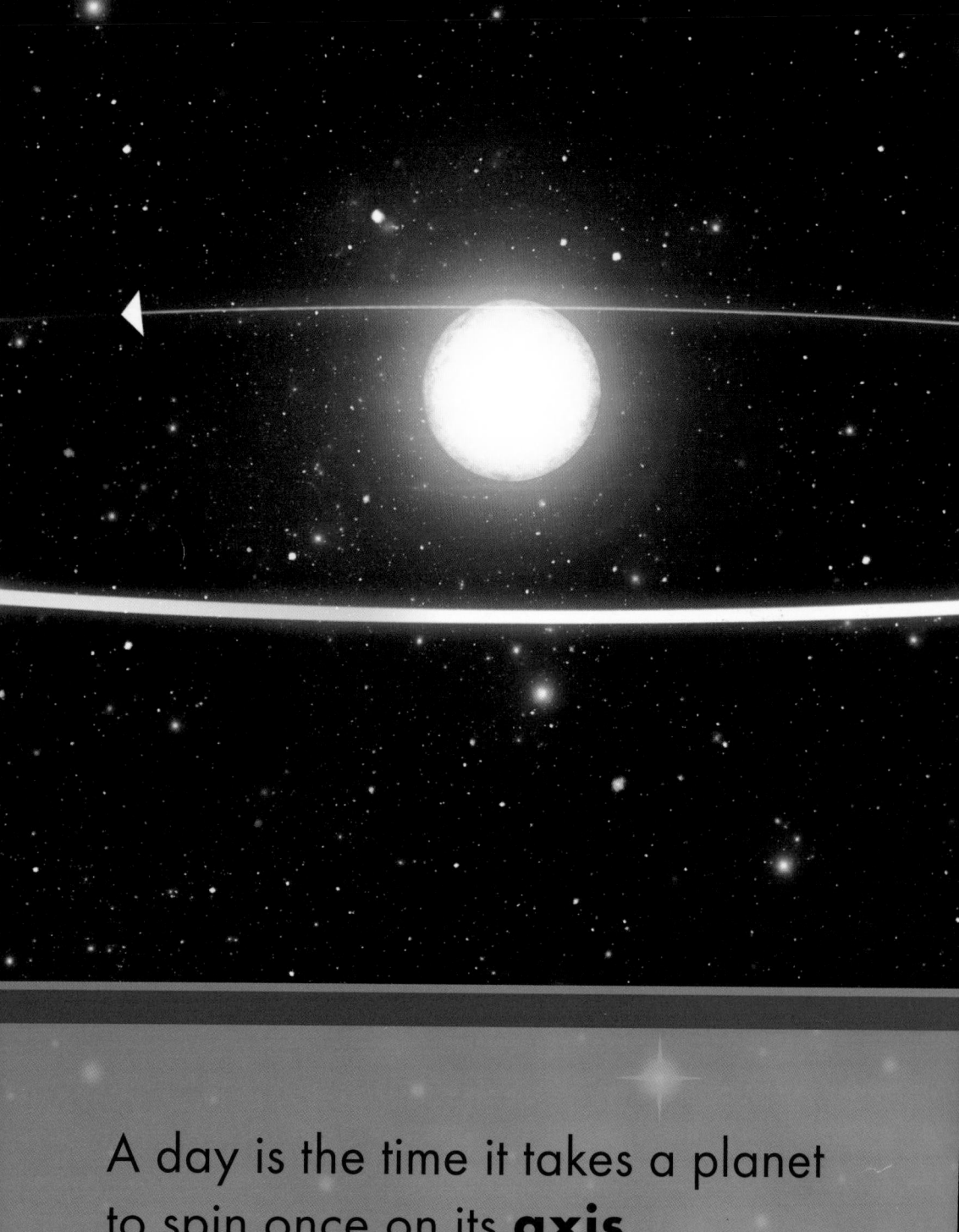

A day is the time it takes a planet to spin once on its **axis**.

axis

A day on Jupiter is about 10 Earth hours long.

Jupiter has a wide range of temperatures. It is -230° Fahrenheit (-145° Celsius) in the upper **atmosphere**.

upper atmosphere

core

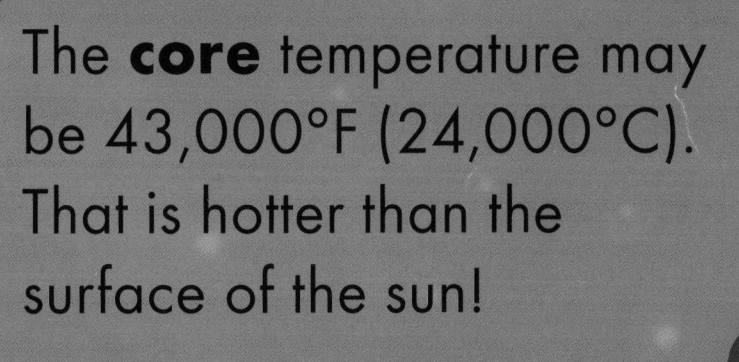

The **core** temperature may be 43,000°F (24,000°C). That is hotter than the surface of the sun!

Great Red Spot

The range of temperatures causes storms on Jupiter. The biggest storm is the **Great Red Spot**.

Scientists think this storm is 350 years old. The storm winds can reach 225 miles (360 kilometers) per hour.

Different gases give Jupiter its many colors. Bands of red, blue, brown, and white line the planet.

Jupiter has three **rings**. They are made of dust. The largest ring is 20 miles (30 kilometers) thick.

Astronomer

Galileo Galilei discovered Jupiter's biggest **moons** in 1610. These moons are Callisto, Europa, Io, and Ganymede.

Europa

Galileo Galilei

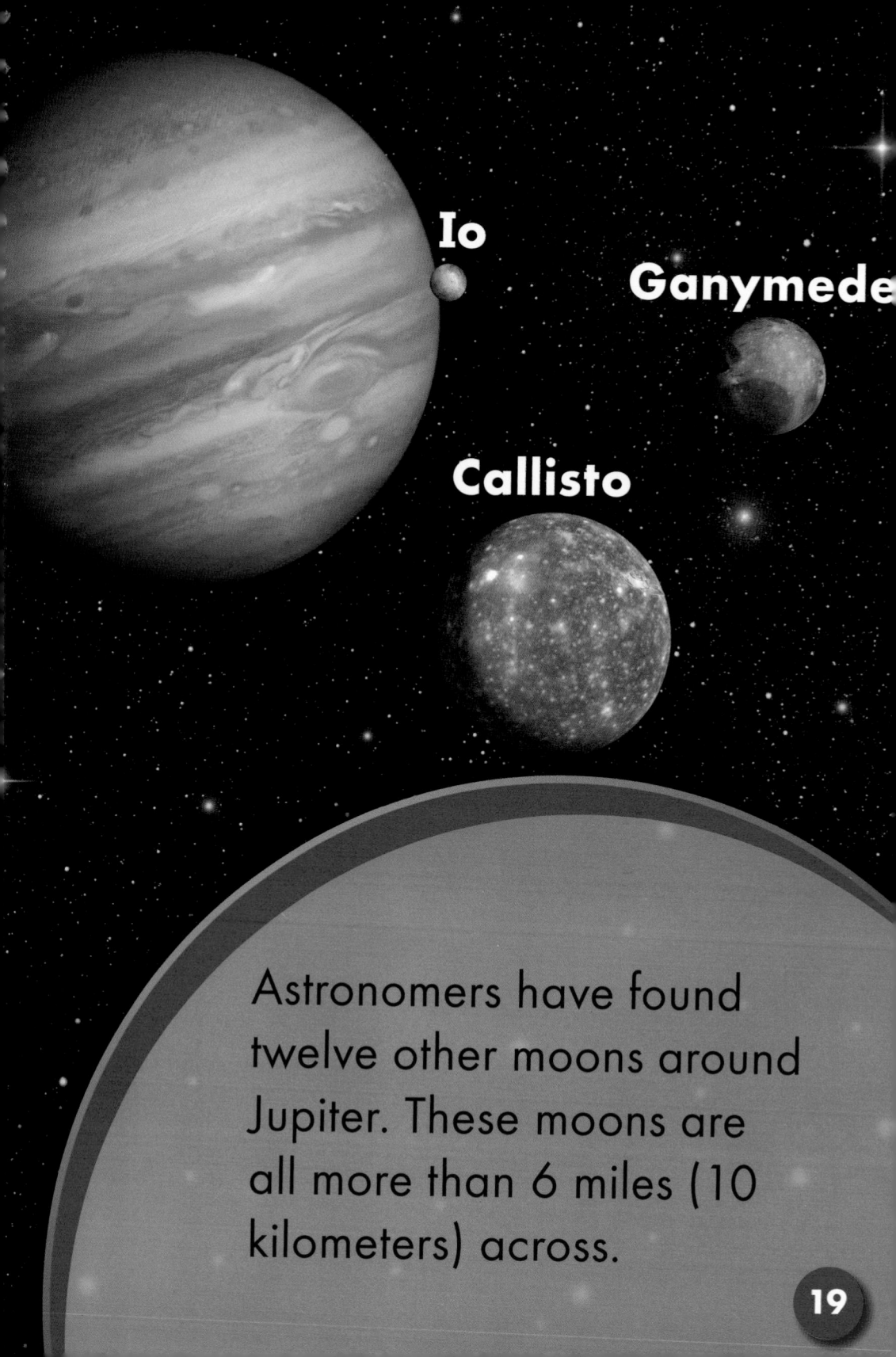

Io

Ganymede

Callisto

Astronomers have found twelve other moons around Jupiter. These moons are all more than 6 miles (10 kilometers) across.

Scientists have sent **space probes** to Jupiter. Some probes have taken photos of Jupiter.

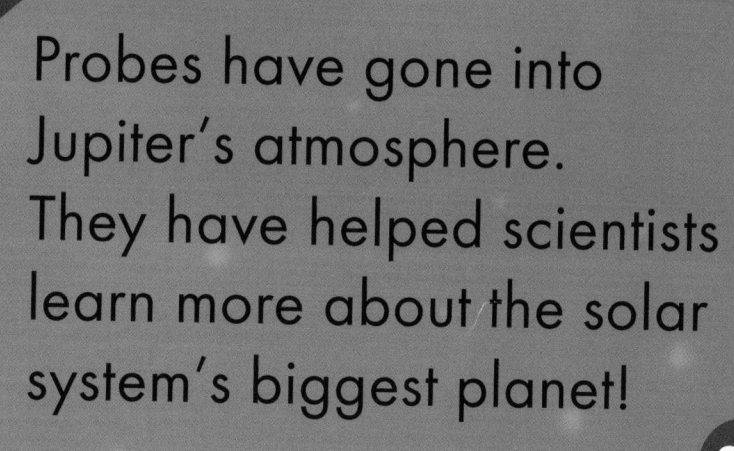

Probes have gone into
Jupiter's atmosphere.
They have helped scientists
learn more about the solar
system's biggest planet!

Glossary

astronomer—a scientist who studies space and objects in space

atmosphere—the gases around an object in space

axis—an imaginary line that runs through the center of a planet; a planet spins on its axis.

core—the center of a planet

gas giant—a planet made up mainly of gas instead of rock

Great Red Spot—a large storm in Jupiter's atmosphere that looks like a big red spot

moons—space objects that orbit a planet or other space object

orbit—to travel around the sun or other object in space

planet—a large, round space object that orbits the sun and is alone in its orbit

rings—flat bands made of pieces of rock, dust, and ice that form around a planet; rings look solid from far away.

Roman god—a god worshipped by the people of ancient Rome; Jupiter was the god of thunder.

solar system—the sun and the objects that orbit it; the solar system has planets, moons, comets, and asteroids.

space probes—spacecraft that explore planets and other space objects and send information back to Earth; space probes do not carry people.

To Learn More

AT THE LIBRARY

Landau, Elaine. *Jupiter*. New York, N.Y.: Children's Press, 2008.

Simon, Seymour. *Destination: Jupiter*. New York, N.Y.: HarperCollins, 2000.

Taylor-Butler, Christine. *Jupiter*. New York, N.Y.: Children's Press, 2008.

ON THE WEB

Learning more about Jupiter is as easy as 1, 2, 3.

1. Go to www.factsurfer.com.

2. Enter "Jupiter" into the search box.

3. Click the "Surf" button and you will see a list of related Web sites.

With factsurfer.com, finding more information is just a click away.

BLASTOFF! JIMMY CHALLENGE

Blastoff! Jimmy is hidden somewhere in this book. Can you find him? If you need help, you can find a hint at the bottom of page 24.

Index

The images in this book are reproduced through the courtesy of: Juan Eppardo, front cover, pp. 9 (small), 10-11, 12-13; Timothy Gillis, p. 4 (small); Detlev van Ravenswaay / Science Photo Library, pp. 4-5; Andrea Danti, pp. 6-7; NASA, pp. 8-9, 14 (small), 16, 17; Antonio M. Rosario, pp. 14-15; Bill Sanderson / Science Photo Library, p. 18 (small); Science Photo Library, pp. 18-19; Stephen Girimont, pp. 20-21.

Blastoff! Jimmy Challenge (from page 23).
Hint: Go to page 19 and shoot for the moon.